M000013030

How to Love Difficult People

Receiving and Sharing
God's Mercy

William P. Smith

New
Growth
Press

www.newgrowthpress.com

All Scripture quotations, unless otherwise indicated, are taken from the *Holy Bible*, New International Version®, NIV®. Copyright © 1973, 1978, 1984 by International Bible Society. Used by permission of Zondervan. All rights reserved.

New Growth Press, Greensboro, NC 27429
Copyright © 2008 by Christian Counseling & Educational Foundation. All rights reserved. Published 2008

Cover Design: The DesignWorks Group, Nate Salciccioli and Jeff Miller, www.thedesignworksgroup.com

Typesetting: Robin Black, www.blackbirdcreative.biz

ISBN-10: 1-934885-40-1
ISBN-13: 978-1-934885-40-6

Library of Congress Cataloging-in-Publication Data

Smith, William P., 1965-
   How to love difficult people: receiving and sharing God's mercy / William P. Smith.
      p. cm.
   Includes bibliographical references and index.
   ISBN 978-1-934885-40-6
   1. Conflict management—Religious aspects—Christianity.
   2. Interpersonal relations—Religious aspects—Christianity.
   3. Love—Religious aspects—Christianity. I. Title.
   BV4597.53.C58S65 2008
   248.4—dc22

                                          2008011944

Printed in Canada
. 11 12   6 5

There are people in my world who are hard to love. Some of them are determined to protect themselves; prickly and constantly on the defensive, it only takes something little to set them off. They lash out verbally, and then withdraw emotionally and sometimes physically, cutting off all chance of communication. Others are just plain nasty for no apparent reason. They seem to take perverse pleasure in sabotaging every interaction, so most exchanges end unhappily with hard feelings on both sides. And then there are the Eeyore types who mope through life always looking at the dark side. They notice and (endlessly!) discuss every gloomy detail of their lives. They throw a wet blanket on every conversation. Frankly, I get tired of them all.

How do I deal with difficult people? Sometimes I avoid them by ignoring their emails, losing their telephone messages, or not allowing them to catch my eye at work. Other times I try to manage our interactions by keeping them as short as possible. Occasionally I cope by talking about them with someone else. And when I've just had it, I give them a piece of my mind. Sarcastic, critical, and loud are my preferred options when I'm fed up and can't take it anymore.

Hmm, that's an interesting set of reactions… avoidance, manipulation, gossip, quarreling. You know, when you think about it, I can be pretty difficult to love too.

We Are All Hard to Love

Learning to love difficult people starts with understanding that you (like me) are hard to love too. You might not be difficult to love in the same way as those around you are, and you may not cause the same amount of relational damage; but on the inside, in your own way, you are just as difficult to love as everyone else.

Just like those difficult people, you and I sin

and go astray (Isaiah 53:6; Romans 3:22–23). It took Jesus' sacrifice on the cross for God to welcome you and me into his family. God doesn't love you because you make such a wonderful addition to his family; he loves you in spite of what you are like. And through his love for you, he changes you to be like himself. He makes you lovely, even though you didn't start out lovely (2 Corinthians 5:17, 21). You need exactly the same things from God—grace, mercy, kindness, and welcome—that others need from you.

If deep down you know you are unlovable *and* God's acceptance of you is completely undeserved, then you will have a welcoming attitude toward other unlovely people. But if you believe you're basically a decent person who anyone would be privileged to know, then you won't welcome others until they get their act together and become decent…just like you!

Learning the difficult skill of loving difficult people starts by asking God to show you how hard you are to love. When he answers your prayer, ask him to forgive you. Then because you have been forgiven for so much, you will be able to share the grace you have received with others (Luke 7:47).

Have God's Goals for Difficult Relationships

Think about how God treats difficult and prickly people. He pursues his people much more earnestly than they have ever pursued him. He isn't put off by their difficult and prickly natures. And when he captures our hearts, he transforms us to be like himself. It is now our privilege and calling to imitate God by pursuing others so they too will know God's love.

This means adopting God's goals for your difficult relationships. If your goal in pursuing others is that, at some point, they will be nicer to you or easier to be around, then your relationships are already on shaky ground. Trying to get someone to treat you the way you want to be treated makes manipulation the foundation of your relationship.

Your goal for difficult people should be the same as God's goal: that they become all that God wants them to be. When you do this, you are pursuing them in the same way God does. You are siding with God in what he is doing in his universe. The results may not be exactly what you'd like, but there is no better person to work with and for!

How Does God Pursue People?

To be used by God in these difficult relationships, you need to understand how he pursues people. How is it that the all-powerful God of the universe doesn't terrify us when he comes looking for us? Why don't we run the other way? Part of the reason is that God has an established track record of being involved in his people's lives for their good.

Think back to the Garden of Eden where God responded to Adam and Eve's rebellion by promising a Deliverer who would free us from our slavery to sin (Genesis 3:15). God remembered that promise for thousands of years and never turned his back on his people, even though they turned away from him many times. Instead, he continued to move all history toward the point when, at just the right time, Jesus stepped onto center stage (Galatians 4:4).

Jesus literally went to hell and back for you. His death guarantees your forgiveness; his resurrection guarantees your new life; and his Spirit guarantees that he will never leave you. Jesus has remained faithful to you, even through the many times you have not loved him with all your heart, soul, mind, and strength. He is committed to you for the long haul.

He invites you to run to him to find safety. Glance quickly through the Psalms and notice the many different ways God invites you to think of him as your protector. He is your rock, fortress, refuge, stronghold, shield, and strong tower (Psalms 9:9; 18:2; 94:22; 144:2). He invites you to find safety in him.

He gives you confidence in his invitation by showing you how he has treated people who were having a hard time trusting him. The stories of Abraham questioning God's promise (Genesis 15), Gideon doubting God's call (Judges 6—7), and Elijah running from Jezebel (1 Kings 19) show you a God who pursues fainthearted people gently and kindly. It's God's gentleness and kindness that moves them closer to him. He does not handle people roughly—not even those who doubt him.

As you watch God engage people in the Bible, you learn that he really doesn't treat us as our sins deserve (Psalm 103:10). He doesn't pursue us to make us pay him back for all our sins and mistakes. He wants us to turn to him and be reconciled to him (2 Corinthians 5:20–21).

Are you beginning to see God's heart for people? He does not engage people with a hidden agenda to make his life easier. He invests himself in relationships that make his life harder!

Doing so certainly brings him glory, but it is not an impersonal glory displayed on a museum wall for us to line up and inspect. Instead, it's a glory that leaps off the canvas, personally touching you and me. When you experience this kind of glory, you are drawn into a relationship that's beyond your wildest dreams. His glory alters you so that you reflect him in the way he intended from creation. As you are changed to reflect God, you will want to pursue the difficult people in the same way God pursued you.

Practical Strategies for Change

Pursuing people the way God does means sharing with them the same mercy, love, kindness, and welcome that God has shared with you. Yes, there are things you'll probably need to confront in them, *but* just like between you and Jesus, that confrontation needs to take place within the context of a relationship. Here are some things to do that will help you build that kind of caring relationship with the difficult people in your life.

Admit Your Own Failings

The apostle Paul was handpicked by Jesus to see his resurrected body; he was used by God to share the gospel all over the known world; and wherever he preached churches were started. Why then does he keep reminding us of his failings—that he was a blasphemer, a persecutor of Christians, and an enemy of Jesus (1 Timothy 1:12–17)? He doesn't do this just once; he regularly and publicly proclaimed his failings (Acts 22:3–5; 1 Corinthians 15:9; Galatians 1:13; Philippians 3:6).

Paul had two reasons for his public confessions: to give glory to God and to give hope to others. Paul highlighted his sins to throw an even brighter spotlight on Jesus, his Rescuer. His message was, "If Jesus can do this for me, the chief of sinners—a self-righteous, murdering, religious hypocrite—then surely he can do the same for you!" Paul's confession inspires hope. In the same way, when I admit my own failings and point out how Jesus has worked in me, others realize I am no better than they are. This gives them hope that God is also at work in them.[1]

Pursue Others for Their Sake

One of the most selfless stories in the Bible is when Moses threw himself between God and the people of Israel. God told Moses that he was going to destroy the Israelites because they were worshiping a golden calf. In a moment that anticipates Christ's self-forgetting ministry, Moses throws himself in the gap, interceding for his wayward people (Exodus 32:11–13).

I am always struck by how dangerous it was for Moses to stand between an angry God and the objects of his wrath. *And* I'm challenged by how Moses' action guaranteed that his life would be harder because he would be stuck leading obstinate, rebellious people. How much easier his life would have been if he had let God wipe them out! But Moses was motivated by God's glory and the people's plight, not by his own interests. That same kind of self-sacrificing interest for others should also be the motivation in our relationships.[2]

Do you believe God wants to use you in someone else's life for their good? Remember, it was God who appointed Moses to lead the Israelites. Do you think that appointment was accidental? God knew the future, so he knew that one day Moses would stand in the gap between him and his people. In the same way he also appointed Christ to rescue you. Now, since you are a Christian, he appoints you to be in places where you can help to rescue others.

So begin by asking, "What does this other person *need?*" instead of "What do they *want?*" or "What do *I want* from him or her?" Then determine how you can act to help provide for their needs.

Involving yourself with others usually doesn't make life easier. Instead, it nearly always guarantees that your life will be more difficult. Realizing that all your needs are truly met in Christ will keep you from expecting too much from others as your care for them.

Point Out Areas of Growth

When I am tired of other people's sin, they tend to shrink to the single dimension of being sin-on-two-legs.[3] Then I become very good at pointing out all the wrong things they do. This sets up a dynamic where they fail, I criticize, they try to have less to do with me (failing again!), which I criticize, etc.

I have found that it makes a huge difference to this downward relationship spiral when I realize that people are not one-dimensional. If the other person is a Christian, then he has the Holy Spirit at work in him. But even if the person is not a Christ follower, he is still created in God's image and, although fallen, still has traces of God's image.

What does this theological truth mean practically? It means that when you notice how critical you are, you need to make it your goal to catch others doing things right. Start by repenting for preferring to see only the evil in others, then spend time looking (sometimes this is hard work!) for what is positive in others and draw their attention to it. You are simply seeking to communicate, "I am not your enemy. I am for you! I am on your side." Often that shift in your attitude and approach to others has an important healing effect on strained relationships.

Love Cares about What's Best for Others

The bottom line in loving difficult people—actually in loving all people!—is realizing that love acts to care for the other person's best interests. Love requires you to extend yourself toward another to do what that person needs without worrying about what you may or may not receive in return.

To understand what loving someone like this looks like, think about it in the context of a marriage relationship. How do you love your spouse if she ignores you or only pays attention to you when she wants something? It's not wrong for you to want interaction with your spouse. It's easy to feel alone if you are living with someone who withdraws and hides from you or lashes out and attacks. A desire for companionship is not wrong. Amazingly, in the Garden of Eden before sin entered the world, Adam had perfect communion with God, but he was also alone in a way that was not good (Genesis 2:18).

It doesn't seem wrong to hope for a return when you've extended yourself to others. Is it wrong? Well … honestly, that depends.

Loving, reciprocal relationships are gifts from God. They are neither earned nor deserved. That means it's appropriate to look for a response and even to ask for one, but you cannot think of a response as a payback for how you've treated the other person. Nor can you demand it. When your desire for a response from your spouse changes into a demand, it becomes an ugly, grasping thing that actually ruins any chance of relationship (James 4:1–3).

Another helpful way to think about it is to flip-flop the emphasis. Do you see how dangerous it is for your spouse to not respond to you? You feel isolated in your marriage, but do you see how your spouse is being harmed by not connecting and giving? Your spouse is remaining emotionally and relationally immature. He is shrinking his soul by not learning to give. And he's setting himself up for a rude awakening both with others and with God by mistakenly believing the world revolves around him.

The second great commandment, "Love your neighbor as yourself" (Mark 12:31), is your guide here. Do you care about the trouble your spouse is in, or can you only see what you're not getting? I'm not saying that you should endlessly give or never confront your spouse's selfishness. But your reasons for doing so need to strongly communicate that it's not good for *her* to live the way she is. When you start with love as your goal, you will be able to do good to your spouse while avoiding the pitfalls of bitterness and anger.

Love Endures for the Long Haul

We can get tired pretty quickly of caring about someone more than we do ourselves. This happens to me often. There are so many times when I feel worn out by someone else. When that happens, I flip open my Bible and read Romans 15:5–6. Paul is talking about living in harmony with one another, and then he asks for help from "the God who gives endurance and encouragement."

Notice how those two elements—endurance and encouragement—work together. When you'd like to stop trying to reaching out to a difficult person, God enables you to endure, to keep on plugging even when things are rocky between you.

But he's more than a God of endurance. If that's all God is, then you might easily feel like you have a god of drudgery who is joyless and dark, and forces you to walk down rough relational roads with no relief in sight.

Thankfully, you worship a different God. Your God is a God of encouragement. Your God brings light and joy to your soul as you strive to bring him glory through your relationships. The road of relational harmony is difficult (you will need this God of endurance!), but it's not bleak because he is an encouraging God.

So when you are ready to quit, you need to ask him to encourage you. Let him remind you that because he is for you, no one can be against you (Romans 8:31). Hear from him again that Jesus gave up his life for you, and he fully intends to finish the work he began in you.

He has not given up on you, although you know he has every reason to. It's his encouragement that will move you to repent of your self-focus and give you the desire to try again with others.

This sounds great, but you and I both know how hard it is to do. When you notice how difficult really loving others is, you need to remember and experience once again all the riches that are already yours in Christ. You have a present relationship with him! He has given you so much relational wealth that you can readily afford to give it away. And since you are giving out of your excess, you don't need to wheedle a handout from anyone else. If you catch yourself doing that, take a moment and pray through Ephesians 3:14–19:

For this reason I kneel before the Father, from whom his whole family in heaven and on earth derives its name. I pray that out of his glorious riches he may strengthen you with power through his Spirit in your inner being, so that Christ may dwell in your hearts through faith. And I pray that you, being rooted and established in love, may have power, together with all the saints, to grasp how wide and long and high and deep is the love of Christ, and to know this love that surpasses knowledge— that you may be filled to the measure of all the fullness of God.

Ask Jesus to fill your heart with the knowledge of the breadth, length, height, and depth of his love for you. Ask him to fill you with joy in the inheritance you already have from him. As he answers that prayer, you will be able to genuinely love the difficult people in your life.

Endnotes

1. For an extended discussion of Paul's public confession, see my book *Caught Off Guard* (Greensboro, NC: New Growth Press, 2007) Chapter 18.

2. For an extended discussion of Moses' intercession, see my book *Caught Off Guard*, Chapter 12.

3. This is Paul Tripp's phrase, which I've never been able to better.

If you were encouraged by reading this booklet, perhaps you or someone you know would also be blessed from these booklets:

Angry Children: Understanding and Helping Your Child Regain Control, by Michael R. Emlet, M.Div., M.D.

Breaking Pornography Addiction: Strategies for Lasting Change by David Powlison, M.Div., Ph.D.

Controlling Anger: Responding Constructively When Life Goes Wrong by David Powlison, M.Div., Ph.D.

Divorce Recovery: Growing and Healing God's Way by Winston T. Smith, M.Div.

Eating Disorders: The Quest for Thinness by Edward T. Welch, M.Div., Ph.D.

Facing Death with Hope: Living for What Lasts by David Powlison, M.Div., Ph.D.

Family Feuds: How to Respond by Timothy S. Lane, M.Div., D.Min.

Freedom from Addiction: Turning from Your Addictive Behavior by Edward T. Welch, M.Div., Ph.D.

Freedom from Guilt: Finding Release from Your Burdens by Timothy S. Lane, M.Div., D.Min.

Healing after Abortion: God's Mercy Is for You by David Powlison, M.Div., Ph.D.

Help for Stepfamilies: Avoiding the Pitfalls and Learning to Love by Winston T. Smith, M.Div.

Help for the Caregiver: Facing the Challenges with Understanding and Strength by Michael R. Emlet, M.Div., M.D.

Help! My Spouse Committed Adultery: First Steps for Dealing with Betrayal by Winston T. Smith, M.Div.

Helping Your Adopted Child: Understanding Your Child's Unique Identity by Paul David Tripp, M.Div., D.Min.

To learn more about CCEF visit our website at www.ccef.org.